Misery Erection

A Book ov Haiku

penned by

Caius Domitius Veiovis

Misery Erection

A Book ov Haiku

Gralok Publishing
1st Edition
Trade Paperback

ISBN: 978-1-7378513-9-4
Literature & Fiction › Poetry

INTRODUCTION

This is what happens when the Void finds Buddha and starts journaling. When a man feeds his enlightenment through a meat grinder and binds it with duct tape and perseverance. But what bleeds across these pages isn't the rage one might expect. There's outrage, yes, both righteous and precise, but what lingers is raw insight.

This collection shows what it means when an unbound mind endures inside caged conditions, when the human spirit, throttled and cornered, still finds ways to create, to excel. It captures the moments when a bound man reaches through barbed time and communes with the old cycles. There's no real civility here, just field notes scrawled in shadow and alienation. If anything here shocks you, that's no fault of the work itself, it's just a testament to how little you know the man.

So if you came looking for grace, you're in the wrong temple. The monks here burn their robes and smoke the ashes.

"Editor"-

Gralok Loptsson (August 2025)

PROLOGUE

Zen masters and drunks, wanderers, vagrants, anarchists, suicides and finger snapping bohemian freaks....Haiku!

There is a tradition in the literary world, most revered among the lunatic fringe — among the iconoclasts, the psychonauts, the punk rock assassins and bootlaced queers., One that holds firm and will NEVER falter — To set the flames ov liberation to ALL traditions which would hinder the free development ov artistic expression and the true individual spirit! And then ov course there are those, the starch necked Conservatives, elitist hipster trendies, flag waving political pigs, straights, scholars and other prudish dogmatists, who would dismiss outright any and all forms ov art which transgress the boundaries, so carefully set, that define, constrict and enforce a passive conformity upon the individual sovereign will. Boundaries, CHAINS, which are designed and manufactured to enslave us! But then — we're not talking about petty dualisms here! Its really not as simple as counter posing GG Allin and Taylor Swift, William S. Burroughs and Dear Abbey!, though eye would argue that the raw, filth smeared, nakedness ov the one — is a damning commentary upon the squeaky clean "high fashion" ov the other. And THIS is where we find it!, Yeah, "IT" — the purest ov all doses!, the visceral, nerve igniting truth that kicks you in the fukking kunt like a nitro boosted Brujeria Brew right out ov the primordial jungle!!!   It's easy to get caught up in the mix ov many words. Twisting, turning, meandering, superfluous snares — rife with ulterior motives, hidden meanings and subliminal moralisms which presuppose an agreed upon social contract., the fine print, Man — those hard to make out lines that say you just signed your life away for a good credit rating! THOSE lines!!! — CUT THE LINES!!!! cut it ALL down and cut it ALL out! NOW!!! And tell me — What do YOU have left?

   Caius Domitius Veiovis W 105269 — North Central Correctional Institution, 2025

Misery Erection

Leaving this place alive?

    perhaps —

  i'm already dead

                So silent

                  the evening mist

             and the voice ov Buddha

Hot cup ov coffee! —

  This cell

    is freezing

                As i lay here in bed

                  holding my cock —

                A return to infancy

New Years day?

　　The crow takes little notice —

grey skies

　　　　　　　　There is only NOW

　　　　　　　　Bloodred Sunset

　　　　　　　　　there IS only now

Dead bird in the grass

Nope!

just a leaf

　　　　　　　　　Next year

　　　　　　　　i'll hang myself —

　　　　　　　　Maybe.

Passing by

our eyes meet —

Hir smile vanishes

A hunger

knowing No satiety —

The passing seasons

As the day bleeds out

my thoughts return —

 ever to you

Winter storm

No way out

The Gate is closed!

My body now roams

where my mind only wandered —

Unleashed!!!

Horizon lost

Earth and Sky a blinding white.

The Storm

Woven with old string

The scent ov wet dog —

My dreadlocks

Edging forward

to some longed for desire...

What was it again?

My balls

like two frozen eggs —

The Cold Cell

                              Footprints fading

                    in this world ov transience —

                              Every door is open!

Starry Night

unblinking —

Longing for...

                              Crow feathers

                    hanging on the wall —

                              Take flight!

                                                    15

The Buddha on my shelf

does not seem to notice

He is in prison

                Hir touch...

                    A memory —

                i will never possess

The smell ov Jasmine,

and other things

   —i'd rather forget.

                Thinking about suicide

                    i hear it calling —

                      The Ocean

A crow in the pines

  "It's warm for January"

Prison yard

        -On Basho:
          Insensitive Bastard!!!

       i'd have taken the girls with me —

          Bush Clover and The Moon.

Begging for food

The squirrel blocks the walkway —

A furry little monk

          Fresh grass

        Cutting through the snow —

           No struggle

Soggy tofu

    and a bitter apple.

Such fortune!

                Though locked in this cage

                i remain

                a traveler

Shit on my dick

And not for the fist time —

Prison sex

                In this floating world,

                so full ov anguish and loss —

                Sipping tea.

"The Ear"

His finest work!

23rd ov December

On love —

She speaks ov commitment...

No thanks!!!

Driving snow and lightening

Strange figures carved in the drifts —

Night Storm.

Fasting for the day

Because it crossed my mind —

A kiss for Tara.

The reality ov my life

is like the wind through the trees

                    Righteously stoned

                    i float down the hallway —

                    Waxed linoleum

Starry Night

reflecting upon my meditations —

She laughs

                    Sweeping the cell

                    and plucking ants from the dust pile.

                    Be free my friends!

20

Someone to hold —

Another dream,

Another night alone

My days,

filled with elusive tension,

are empty

Bluejay in the spruce

screeching at me —

"Back off!!!!"

A leashed dog

such casual cruelty

Lonely with my haiku

  No one to share with —

    Alienated joy

        Callous compassion?

          — spitting candy on the floor

            to feed the ants

Cold December

A sunless afternoon —

High on nutmeg.

        grey skies

          barren trees

            a single raven

"My" cell

Locked from the outside.

"Outside"?

empty stomach

a bed with no mattress —

the cold cell

Turning the lamp on

and off again

Nite haiku

Book ov haiku

dipped in tea

a spontaneous act

Silent Buddha

Meditative and severe

Nothing left to say

                    A mended bowl

                 filled with cool water —

                    My parched lips

i admire the ants —

    wandering aimlessly

        and eating sugar

                    My bed —

                An empty casket.

                    Gypsy

24

Rain in December —

    The cry ov a Bluejay —

Can such things be?

          Cold rain....

          warm for this time ov year —

          A traveler without a coat

sitting cross legged

and again am interrupted —

perhaps for the best

          A kiss denied

          as fingers caress the skin

          ....Sensation

Flies in the showed room

    My friendliest neighbours —

        Don't drown!!!

                White cum in the drain

                  unborn children

                  Cold shower

A perfect Darkness

    No light to obscure my path —

i am truly Dead

                Tibetan New Year

                The sun rises golden

                So fleeting.....

Prison is torture

   Dead —

      and alone among the dead

                  Grinning

                    From the Dark

                      Possum skull

Lotus

anointed in sandalwood oil —

The Void

                  Life, Man!

                  It's all just...

                  Mist.

tiny little skull

looking for my crumbs again?

empty skies

Fragments ov memory

litter the autumn highway —

An old wine bottle

Hanging bones

Symbols ov my existence

This wretched cell

"Om Kreem Kali"

Hir answer —

Silence

Just barely made it

but she did!

The turtle

                                        Twisting

                                        my filthy dreadlocks

                                        at the root

Today becomes the past

the past becomes the future —

Periwinkles

                                        From every seed

                                        to every leaf and branch

                                        A masterpiece

cold dejected me

all walking in slow column

drawn by hunger

                        Within these walls....

                    "The mind is its own place"

                                Prison

Angered by my plight

    Yet the starling overhead

        has no sympathy

                        Dead trees in the fog

                        An unvisited hill —

                        The prison cemetery

Ov matters so small

So much to complain about —

People

An old pond

i flip out my cock —

The sound ov water

lonely

i pretend to be in love

and make a fool ov myself

calling The Goddess

108 times

and then again

No future

No haunting past

The Black Lotus

                         Laurels too pure

                 to adorn these vulgar crags —

                           Though in dreams......

Sipping hot tea

Disinclined to speak ov "things" —

   Brooding

                           Bones in the ground

                       Remembering yesterday

                            The coming dawn

Distracted by fools

   A fool myself!

      —Lost

                  Through shifting

                    ominous clouds —

                  The light!

Hir body

Unseen

My lament

                  Hir spirit

                  Glimpsed

                  My unbound joy

Yellowhaze sunset

Seen through a razor wire fence —

Melting snow.

                    Stepping through the fog

                    Its curtain closing behind me

                    Light dims

Fog —

   Penetrating my bones

      Ethereal

                    A memory....

                    Singing death songs to a dragonfly

                    Summers end

Old washcloth

stiff and hanging

Like a mildewed corpse

"Where one has gone,

others may follow."

Says the prostitute

The dog looked up

questioning my sanity —

No answer

First sip ov coffee —

it hits me

like a shot ov dope!

Warm January afternoon

i stay in my cell —

Feeling antisocial

Facing the new day

Just as horny as yesterday —

Morning wood

In this prison

i practice being a ghost —

Soon enough

A crack in the floor

collecting dust —

This world

Cellmate pissing

i could really do without this!

FLUSH

                    The sting ov rejection

                            or perhaps...

                            Just a mosquito

Being myself

to the dismay ov others —

FUKK OFF!!!

                    Another bridge,

                            burned to cinders!

                    One step closer to freedom

The lamp

illuminating only itself

So black the crypt

                    —"i'm screwed!"

                 stating the obvious

                 caught in a tryst

My libido

Kicked into overdrive —

The SIGHT ov hir!

                 "Fukkin Chota!!!"

             Blood splatters the hallway —

                 A typical day in here

Perimeter lights

glow eerily through the sleet

Marching to the chow hall

                              Stopped eating fish —

                                  Made the decision

                                  Not to decide

Everything's alright

        all the time —

    This waking nightmare

                              Another nite

                              at one —

                        Under the Thousand Stars

The pigeons

   there again the next day —

Mendicants all!

                    Sense ov self fades

               "Internal" and "External"

                      Only shadow

Trying to stay warm

   under my flimsy blanket —

      No success

                    Listening to

            "The ol' Diamondback Sturgeon"

                Tears streak down my face

A whores bath —

   This fine morning

Who deserves better?

                                          sitting here

                                            alone —

                              a conversation with friends

Slate blue sky

   crystal splinters

      falling

                                        Another day gone —

                                            Gone?

                                    It was never here

Meeting with a pretty girl —

    hir eyes

  so distracting

                      She looks at me

                          and walks away —

                      Nothing said

The Guru

    The Seeker —

Speech falters

                      Not held in the hands —

                          Hir memory

Closing my eyes

    to see things clearly —

  What foolishness!

                  Leaving tracks in the snow

                 The rabbit,

                who will eat my garden

Piercing my navel

  Couldn't get the ring through —

Coitus Interruptus

                 The Night —

                Gleaming black

                 as bright as the sun!

The rivers we speak ov

   are only metaphors —

      It's all in your head

                    Sick ov this intolerance

                        i step away

                            from myself

A chance meeting

   on the lonely road —

Nepenthe

                  Sting ov the needle

                  Process ov Becoming

                  World without end, Amen

Through the fog

    Languidly flowing —

        Breath

                Gun towers

            Razor wire fences

          Yet my mind is free

Calling through the mist

    A murder ov crows

        October

                cold and damp

          mending my tattered shoes —

                nowhere to go

Boiled tofu

   again.....

The chickens are lucky!

              Hassan called the shots

              "Nothing is true..." —

              THAT was a lie

¡Neuvo Testamento¡

   Sorry kid

     We're closed

              So fukkin tired

              ov all this inane talk —

              Rainbows on the water

Cellmate snoring

Stomach growling

No sleep

Healing —

Contemplating my navel

infection

Unannounced

realization —

The day HAS NOT blown by!

Creeping suspicion

This broad has a vagina!

Disappointment

The time i've spent jerking off

   seems like

      infinity

            Upon arrival

              recognition

            ov predatory hunger

In the dark —

 Falling snow

White as little ghosts

            Here are the rules

            There ARE no rules

            Disregard this announcement!

Whatever that is —

    Enlightenment cums

and then smokes a cigarette

                              Pierced through

                                hir bleeding lips

                           Speaking in tongues

Spinning in reverse

    i sit Zazen

and chant to Kali Ma

                              Seeking experience

                            only to lose focus —

                                  Purple sky

My tattoos

each with their own lives —

No separation

i cum on a rag

chew toy for the pig girl

she has a small dick

Red biohazard bag

its contents

appetising

3am

my mind reflects

the clarity ov........

Sleepless delirium

lost wisdom

given to the nite

Bellybutton ring

Crusty and healing

in the early morning gloom

Many layers

created from one —

The folded blanket

Groundhog Day

Birds in the air —

What the fukk IS this!?!

Frantic!

Spawned by my infection —

Dreams become nightmares

On the withered path —

Going somewhere?

Lichen covered stone

Crows

and Mexicans

Screaming at each other

A pink sky

Seen through undressed branches —

Awaiting the Equinox

No longer searching

for The End —

    Broken road

                Beads around my neck

                  All is not vanity

Shivering

Too stubborn to dress warmly

Shivering

                Dancing silhouettes

                  yellow sun

                    reaching for....

Warm one minute

   Freezing my dick off the next —

New England

               My tattooed body

          Unencumbered by clothing

             Primitive and free

The frozen ground —

    it trembled.

   Beneath my feet

             Breadline pigeons

        all fluffed up against the cold

              — Afternoon

A smile

   as the air ov panic spreads —

Late schedule

        The Hunger —

         Darkness blossoms into light?

         Only an illusion

The pain that i feel

is the true emptiness

      Ov being

        Grace personified

       Motionless against blue sky —

        Hawk as Emperor

Hawk

Motionless against the blue sky —

Emperor

                                Stayed inside all day

                                got my dick sucked —

                                  Nothing special

An unhealthy disconnect

  haven't even LOOKED outside!

 These walls

                                Staring at the wall

                            like some freak Bodhidharma —

                                  Get me a gun!!!

Right here and now

  is where i take my chances —

A Wanted Man

              "Villain!"

               They scream from tattered sofas —

                My world don't count for you, Man!!!

i keep hearing about "life"

  but i'm just not seeing it —

The Cell

                Wandering, wandering —

                 This place ov confinement

                   cannot hold me

Locked up, for now

   Though outside The Law

      FOREVER!

           Count Time again

        got this pig lookin' at me....

           FUKK OFF!!!

Clearly depressed

disassociative and angry —

   Yellow sun

           Anti-Social

        Personality Disorder —

          Misdiagnosis

The mail came

    with not a thing for me —

Sick ov writing anyway

              Leave all the essentials behind —

                  especially hir!

Laying here in my rack

    inducing a foot cramp

        Smiling

              You can't walk this off!!!

                Over the horizon —

                  another mirage

No pistol to shoot myself

   and i don't feel like hanging....

      Today

           Moonlight

            it trickles through the fence —

            so quite

Zombies everyfukkingwhere!!!!

   And i'm STILL waiting

      for the Apocalypse?

            Alienated —

              Sitting in the dark

                taking it all in

Looking through my window

once again —

The toothless whore

Prone to madness

driven by lust —

Pax Vobiscum

in the darkness

alone and beleaguered

i remember hir scent

They know

Yet they still to tolerate me —

Friends i hate

In doleful tones repeated —

"We have come to an end"

at every new beginning

Dropped from exhaustion

in the search for Divinity

and lifted My Self

hir laugh contrived

a false smile —

Love

The Lamp

Its flame extinguished

Forever

light fades

  in the cold afternoon —

    winter skies

      Talk ov the Townie

    "Blah, blah, blah, blah, blah, blah, blah." —

     FLUSH THIS TOILET!!!!!!

Pen in hand

all my creative juices

go down the drain

      There it is!

      For my entire life —

      Nothing.

They avoid my eyes

    walking past

        with heads bowed

                    Once borne on the wind

                        an Autumn leaf

                       Stuck in the fence

stranded

    too many obligations —

  mothballed luggage

                    Saturday mourning

                    She went to a funeral

                    Was it mine?

Deep in the west

    sun glittering red

        through miles ov razor wire

                My eyes

              Painted black —

                  Your apparition

Springtime —

    She left the cemetery...

 Hir skull anyway.

              Distant sun

            The ground thaws —

              Muddy boots

There is one chick

  i'd switch it all up for

      and it ISN'T you!

                Lost in my thoughts

                Lost in this world —

                Such is bliss!

Humanity!?!

  Anything but humane

Cannibals all

            Watching the bee

            move from flower to flower —

            Feeling promiscuous

Alone —

Scouring this wasteland,

the vultures circle

Spring thaw

Nothing much ov it

Muddy shoes

The fly has no shame

Swimming through the air

Naked

Bloodied hand —

The once leashed dog

has attained enlightenment

eclipse ov the sun

   from my cell window —

a finch, struggling with a crab apple

           The puddle

              like a Buddha

          in its morning reflections

Pissing me off

   a fat insecure pig bitch

i will not conform

               the grove

            seen through thick fog

              a haunting presence

eyeing me askance

little bird dips hir feathers —

Publick Puddle

Old crow

Dead tree

The sun is shining in the west.

Perfuming my balls

in hopes ov a visitor —

Life is vanity

agony

In the pale mourning

my wisdom (tooth)

69

not enough torture

 so i quit drinking coffee

   again

                    doing time

                In the middle ov nowhere —

                 good song!!!

Some kind ov Bardo

         this day

    or another

                    Contemplating my navel —

                      covered in blood

even the light

is enthralled by hir laughter —

  i've never smiled before

                With the sun on my face

                contemplating suicide —

                    Barefoot

The path is treacherous

  yet there is only one way

Kaos

                  All the worlds woes

                on hir skinny shoulders —

                    contagion

an empty bush

   full ov riotous birds

the landscape white and tranquil

         Pile ov toenails

           yellow and fungal —

        i hear a child's laughter

Spring rain and snow

   the squirrels hide in their nests —

     i am saddened

        I watch a tiny bird

         pulling a worm from the ground.

Tall grass

    cut short without mercy —

Such is life

                in the mud

                filling with water

                    an old footprint

Out ov hibernation

    the human throng —

Year ov The Wood Dragon

                Without hir

             none ov this would be real —

                  "real"?

Pondering life

   i sacrifice my children

      and flush

                 The way out ov this prison

             is NOT through the door —

               but i'll take it!

for You my prayers

for You my love —

Maha Kali, cum to me!!!

             lone silhouette

          against the dawns horizon —

             is it me?

Spring was here

   now it's winter, once again —

i could puke!

                  names forgotten

                   faces melding

                 the people we've met

Looked in the puddle

and saw myself there

wriggling in the mud

                 Looked in the puddle

                 and saw YOU there

                 wriggling in the mud

a cloudy mirror

   this puddle in the road

mournful reflections

                        reached into the puddle

                           and found a nickel!

                        what else is in there?!

DOVE in the puddle

and cracked my fukking head —

   Prone to foolishness

                           sat in the puddle

                        for no reason at all —

                           content

Satori!

Pissing in the puddle

              Sucked up the puddle

              Stretched out my arm

              Found Nirvana

Amida Buddha

eyes bleeding virulent rot —

He is black as Death

              Alone at nite

                cellmate in hospital

                i didn't do it!

first rays ov dawn

that is enough

So long in this cell

Yet they know —

They know!!!

My attraction —

a blade to my own throat

dragging slowly

Laughing in my heart

No Law

only Love

Unbeknownst to me

    i was born on this planet —

Who says?

                       Life in prison —

                           reruns

                       ov old stock footage

counting my mala

 i remember

there is nothing to forget

                       it's unhealthy

                        all this inane babble

                       deterioration

lizard

drying on the hot pavement —

no one mourned

                                    hir ass cheeks

                                two obsidian coconuts

                                what strange pleasures

A "Crime" he called it

"against human dignity" —

Fukk the Catholic Church!!!

                                    still i listen

                                    hour after hour

                                to the ringing ov the bells

Reluctant

  to get up and piss

another coffee perhaps

        "Veiovis, Visit!"

       Myself (?) Thee Main Attraction —

        This place is a zoo

Haiku

  in the sweltering heat

    wet paper

          in my solitude

        bizarre thoughts do arise

         not ov your kind

To this tyranny

  i will not submit —

This is the will ov The Lord

                    timid onlookers

            they call life a tragedy —

         but just SMELL the roadkill!!!!

     sitting lotus

i resume to die once more

            up from the the cold mud

         she chirps for the first time —

            spring frog

Strawberry wafers —

　　covered in ants.

　　You're welcome my friends!

　　　　　　No destination

　　　　　　No moral conundrums —

　　　　　　Gypsy Road

i listened to an old man

　telling his life story.....

not a single thing was said

　　　　　　The Question

　　　　　　ov guilt or innocence —

　　　　　　and still they question

Dropped a guitar pick

    bone white —

  Lost forever

               between earth

                 and cloud

            these illusions ov life

The light is dim

  or so it seems...

My thoughts return to hir

           "Do the Right Thing."

        NO! and five thousand times NO!

          Vertical the threshold

Laughing in the face ov Death?

  The moon chuckles —

    Contagiously

            Weight ov oppression —

              the feather

                or the heart?

Seen through the swirling fog

  —a dark window

              The little yellow bird

                flew off by itself

                to take a shit

Throughout blue sky

   drift scattered memories

ov a giant

                        Moved today

                          Where to?

                        i do NOT know.

primping for a visit

   no need

  for this anxiety

                        Baby birds

                             singing

                           in a dead tree

Quoting Milton —

  An exchange develops

    i refuse to decipher

            Under the moon

            Summoning the sun

            My body shorn

Cold New Moon breeze

  Out ov the frozen mud —

  Rib bone

            as with lightening

              long seen from afar

            i am stricken

Shaved in a queue

  thinking ov Genghis Khan

    My head

                A lifetime apart

             Though never separate —

          Within these haunted woods

My tattooed hand

  resting upon the Black Book —

    An evil thing

                Naked

                  and why not be?

                Joyous

Scent ov flowers

and ov the coming storm —

My mind is set

little spider

are you invisible?

noonday sun

Abana

at the water fountain —

My life can end now

Clear skies

filled with ominous clouds —

nothing else

long seasons pass

  still lay the bleached bones

    Flowers bloom

                    Twilight deepens

              an old man's tales ov woe —

                I resolve to hang myself

contemplating thusly

  life assumes new meaning —

i will live forever

                    excruciating

                      this illusion ov time

                    and accumulating dust

Approaching an end
   on the circular road —
Indefatigable!!!

                              Runes carved in stone
                                 the deepest ov lakes —
                                     Nights holy reverie

Lunar Moth
   rising into the pines
wet haze ov sunset

                                Black coffee
                                 the rest is incidental

Life —

This is not my rightful home

    Darkness calls

                    twilight hours

              resenting breath itself —

                Malice.

Flowing freely

is there a sexual tension?

No space between us

                Black Lotus

                    attracting flies —

            The Buddha sits laughing

All out ov tune

¡insanity!

without compromise

                                    cool mists

                                        drear morning

                                            faint scent ov ash

Skull on the altar

  Shifting its position

No abnormalities here

                                    Crows follow me

                                like stink on carrion —

                                    Never truly alone

Granite windowsill

  caked in birdshit —

 The fading evening light

           breathing dust

         drenched in arrogance

           my immortal hate

Under the Black Flag

 A life ov rebellion

 Beyond regret

      Primal Anarchy.

    The revolt ov consciousness —

     A Molotov Cocktail!

Vultures circle

   My fat friend yells out

"I'm not dead yet you bastards!"

                         Unrequited love

                         is there any other kind?

                         The smell ov hyacinth

the morning sun

   it's warmth i'll never know

this private Hell

                         distant mystic haze

                         soul obscured

                         my shadow is gone

The art ov Revolution

    is a daily act

        ov Defiance!

                My shadow

           Laid out across the field —

             Towering in death

Courtyard

    dimly it —

  My enemies conspire

             Contrived opposition

           Position shifts to zero —

             The pale moon hovers

Something tragic —

   The old pine

Weary ov its own strength

             from my bunk

             i can feel the ground shake —

             train rolling by

The Dawn breaks

   My erection stands

Magnificent!

             in the shower

             where flies make their home —

             black mould

Open wound

infected and weeping —

    The scent ov Autumn

                raining for days

                  i'm stuck indoors

                without a coat

Come back!

Too quick to pass judgement

On the spider

        She spoke my name

    Though the smile never reached hir eyes —

          i'll take it

the rising sun

    shining through my cell window —

i awoke from a dream

                      Celebrating...

               the vernal equinox —

                    sans friends

Too eager,

    i split the skin!

Soapstone talon

                    My Thoughts

               like fresh piercings —

                    already infected

inadequacy ov the pig

  black can ov pepper spray

 transference

                        dead tree

                           on an old hill

                    they danced in the streets

dirty needles

  and an HIV test —

double negative

                          Spring?

                    i pretty much missed it.

                      The cold cell

Platonic love

  or self immolation?

It seems i've grown old

                         Just for once

                           without the sarcasm

                         Nothing left to say

Crusty sheets

  reflected in the mirror —

Infeccioso Basura!

                         Hot crazy nites

                         Sweating in leather

                         Blitzed out

all eyes on me

   rudely scrutinizing

      and so i show the cock!

               walking for miles

              ending where i began

              nowhere

13 years in now —

   i miss the drugs

      how dearly i miss them!

              green bed ov grass

              i'd gladly trade

              heart ov a gypsy

Filled with nothing

   the desolation ov this place....

  it crowds me

                 Morning dew

          clinging to existence —

             The sun will rise

a single drop —

   the cup is poisoned

            from hidden gloom

         i observe as the green deepens

          soon it will rain

Oppression has a face

  Bad skin —

And a blue uniform!

        i awoke

        to find myself in revolt

        i awoke

four walls

  and one mind

which contains them all

        Black wings

       Sleek with summer rain —

      The sky is shelter enough

Smell ov old wood

    the lonesome house

        Falling

                Walking with friends

                in solitude —

           the warm afternoon sun

apple blossoms

    they took me by surprise —

baby pink

            an eager lover

            hot wind

            breathing heavy and wet

Luxuriant

  in the cloying humidity —

Like a tribal fetish

                  Descending sun

            slithers over the razor wire

               like Promethian flame

desire for hir

  a dream —

a mocking parody ov dream

                 My serpent tongue

           the silver chalice ov Night

               Oblivion

Hir pleasure

My salvation —

Anything

What strange beasts

to have bread the likes ov me

Ex Ungue Leonem

Huge raindrops hit the pool —

Supernova flashes!

True mysticism

Knuckles white

thinking about the government

Spit mingles with dust

balm ov mourning

  green apocalypse

give me highs that never fade

               old memory

          small yellow flowers —

           what was eye saying?

Met with hostility —

  this fat matricide

and his big stupid mouth

           from the carrion bank

         they scratch their nourishment

          four crows

sipping tea

   in the chilly air ov spring —

i am not in Florida!

        New season

         New piercing

          The tip ov my orkish ear

My ear is sore

   though i still clearly hear

The march ov police boots

        RISEN!

         and so my distain —

         A curse upon mankind

Threatening sky

   First touch ov green

The old maple awakens

                    Solitary crow

              calling out for their lover

                    Bereaved

She saw me today

   For the first and thousandth time

And filched my wallet

                    towards the line

                    I gaze defiant

              under police scrutiny

an ant struts by

   taking no notice ov me

      sitting on the pot

                      Fading light

                       Ice covered tree

                         Prism

  without obstruction

stepping through the mist

my eyes see clearly

                She smiles

            handing me my commissary —

               Lady in red

Once past the checkpoint

everything was NOT fine —

Visiting Jeru

Pebbles in the road

We stop to take notice —

Traveling the wastes

The world

a pleasant grave

feathers fell

aimless my travels

yet with each determined step

i arrive

churning black clouds

  reek ov my own sweat

heat lightening

                Channeling the Hun

           certain barbaric proclivities...

              i'm a Motherfukker!!!!

Beneath the veil ov Night

My heart a funeral pyre —

She cums to me

                Once free

                  once again caged

                Ever wandering

Summer heat

  a telling stench —.

Carcass in the razor wire

          On an outstretched limb,

        contemplating the universe —

           only a shadow....

sick ov this old fukk

  wishing he was dead

Yep.

          burning my eyes

           the caustic light

           oh the hated light!

What a laugh!

   Striving to live

We miss the point entirely

               Eyes ov the sage

             Closed in tranquility...

              Sleeping i'd guess

   Full moon —

a cold and violent glare

  seen through the trees

              "Sick Gauges!" —

              "Thanks Bro!"

             So says The Buddha

in this holy place —

somewhere over there somewhere

The Enlightened One sits

                         rain lightly falling —

                              on the ground

                                a penny

sensing treachery

    the ides ov March

i remain unimpressed

                         Oh ravenous termite

                            SURVIVE!!!

                         And eat away these walls

beaming excitement

the dog remembers my face —

one reason to live

Stopping in awe

a cardinal

Vibrant and RED!

seeing hir smile

resets everything —

come again

Finding an apple

frozen in my pocket —

Cruel winds

sweet tea

bitter circumstances

locked in a cage

                        4am

                        Woke up in a cell —

                        With a cold ass

Winter revisited —

   i've never felt so discarnate

                  crystalline fir

               panicked singing ov many birds

                  winter glass

lone sparrow

dark against the golden vault —

a voice so distant

               two crows

                    playing in the morning sun

through wind and snow

  for a cup ov almond milk

improperly dressed

               Desire

             Would that i had a second!

             The kiss ov cold steel

cry ov the Cicada

   this feeling

is ov dread

                        i looked for hir elsewhere

                           and again

                           found no one

calloused fingers

   ripping necro on my bass —

Grond

                         Staring blind

                    to behold the final sunrise

                       No horizon

Some heathen god?

A "Thing" from desert strands?

Wingless angel

In Tibet

time has no meaning —

HERE it's a real bitch!

a morbid stench

somewhere beyond the wire

the "free world" est mort!

crucified

for the sins ov others

no love

autumn chill

the heat ov summer

I rise with the moon

                              my ink

                              a story

                              no one wants to hear

Pale grey eyes, seeking

 the void —

And finding me

                              Sans inhibition

                                No destination —

                          Grande Danse Macabre

A bell rings

Nowhere to go —

 Prison

                              Questioning my Zen

                         Filthy fukking pig bastards!!!

                              Early winter

my reflection

 a hindrance ov becoming —

trapped image

                              Pale bare skull

                         masked in fallen leaves —

                              Sky ov fire

Feeling chilled
  i dream ov being naked
 In the summer sun

                              white bone
                              cold barren ground
                              frozen marrow

dissolution
self transformation
the Void ov being

                              lurking fear
                              Darkness awakens
                                to sleep once again

A funeral pyre

  Beliefs ignite like withered leaves —

    My heart

            Cold shower castration

            A pleasureless grunt emanation

            Fresh cum in the drain

a spider

  committing suicide

    ran under my foot

              experience

              confined

              this cage

Workers return

Slavestate

Hunchbacked

idol

sitting quietly

not a word spoken

Vacant helm

illusion ov order

and a paper lifeboat

Can such things be?

English muffins and Red Bull —

For breakfast!

digging an earwig

   absentmindedly

content with their lot

               Planet Earth!

                 What we need

               is mutiny!!!

Program interference

   ¡CUIDADO!

      The rules have no meaning

                 Sitting Zazen

              everything is better

                on drugs

Sunlight

nudging me awake —

Fukk completely off!!!

crushing hard

un momento por favor —

i'd have a better chance dead!

What a fun charade!

Masks, nailed to faces —

Undisturbed dust

Baphomet

looking down at me

from the wall

took a long walk...

   in a fukking circle!

don't know where

                        imagine

                           a new way to live

                     you only need to kill yourself

blood red sun

   hanging

  in a grey sky

                        dead rat

                           on the track

                           head crushed

tiny insects

  make a home for themselves

on the dying anise

          5am

          drinking coffee

          in bed

Morning Star

  Seen through a barred window —

Illuminatio Mea!

          Spiders nest —

          LIVE!

          And DEVOUR me!!!

got a bad yen

drenched in perspiration

only one way to solve it

                Found alive

            a most intrepid beetle

              On the ceiling

Itching all nite

  wrapped in a chemical gauze

such is bliss

                Saved

            from certain death —

              an inchworm

spider in a jar

an intolerable thing!

i'm no jailer

                    taking some time off haiku —

                            to fukk

and the it happened

   atmospheric shift

the eerie unlight

                        So many personalities

                    All — vying with each other

                        "I" stand alone

reincarnated

   ah,

to be a maggot!

                    old man

              talking about a future —

                they'll never know

radio tower

   blocking my view

      ov the polluted sky

                blue moon —

                couldn't see it

                through the clouds

No expectation?

    As i pick at the scab

'Til it bleeds

                        Old oak

                        Its leaves

                        Turning yellow

They are NO MATCH

for my laser beam eye style —

Pinned out on dope

                        Mind sprung web

                        Vortex

                        i am the spider and the fly

lemon balm hanging —

   on the floor

a dead beetle

                      going to court

                         —their control

                  a tenuous illusion

"did you hear?"

   "no."

  silence

                    bird on the razor wire

                looked around for a minute

                    and fukked off

red sun

sky blue haze

dusk

                    in the dark

                      a serpent

                    a mirror

On the nod

  Neptunian dreams

In between (The Bardo)

                    road closed

                    cracked pavement

                    it just ends

Meditating

enveloped in nausea —

On junk

                              child rapist

                              playing Boccie

                    should get his face crushed in

Hanging mint to dry

   for crimes unknown —

Bodhidharma wept

                              subtle interactions

                              dire consequences

                    my total lack ov cognition

Posed with a question

  Choosing annihilation —

Fall to Rise!

                pile ov dirt

          sticking out ov the ground

              like a hairy mole

telephone line

  going No Place —

das receiver est mort

                Kicking in nicely

                Methadone

                   And mint tea

hollow stump

  dead

filled with trash

                    soaring above

            heedless ov earth and sky

                 the moth

locked inside

  there was a fight

  somewhere

                    my vision —

                a coiled serpent

                  in the darkness

Arachnid hatchlings

   On the cusp ov liberation —

Go forth an consume!

               nursing a headache

                i decided to take a walk

Night descends

   Shadows deepen

      So too my thoughts

               from Elysian fields

                to a charnel house

                  i awake

Sundown

    Creeping up my wall

Deadly spider

                    in court —

                      a daze

                    ov indignation

Camouflaged spider

    but for that...

        We are so alike

                    the life ov a man?

                    for virtue

                      seek the worm!

district attorney

red nosed

slobbering

world ablaze

from slumber to holocaust

endless inferno

its entire life

spent inside a wall —

the spider

summers end

high crescent moon

birds gathering

seasons pass

they come and go

it's all the same

                              Cold reflection

                         A serpents continence

                              Betraying nothing

"good morning"

"greetings earthling!" —

xenomorph

                         Fukk the war on drugs!

                         We fight for our liberty

                              Aces high

sky on fire

   my skin

  cool to the touch

                             another day

                         tumbling not aimlessly

                              into the next

lost MY mind?

Absurdum Infinitum

"I AM" without eyes

                        free —

                    no more the chains ov reason

                       we dance

hard packed sand

   dried cicada

      baking in the sun

                  Nuri-Botoke...

                     He stares at me —

                  Also without eyes

poor little finch

   doomed to die in prison —

      broken wing

                     sitting Zazen

                  contemplating my navel

                     an empty center

                           145

watching a scab form

such trivial needs

soon to fall

Mourning

the loss ov my navel ring

Rejection

dry heals

inspire me to vomit —

fat man in sandals

Phantom images

only shadows

ov self

In appreciation

  thinly veiled —

They ponder the lock

                  dim solace

             affected mirth

       in the strength ov my bonds

  strange encounters

(ejaculations)

   along this road

                on the precipice

            ov an inverted sea

              Undaunted

these buildings

    accursed places

where spirits are sent to die

           evening sun

             hidden

           behind clouds

Key in hand

  feint ov heart —

  My jailers tremble

           even thus enchained

           oh wretched state!

           they fear me

my life

such an odd thing —

in torment in Hell

Horde ov bats

swarm the yard

Night descends

Prison Overcrowding

i

am alone

amorphous shadows

all out ov proportion

in the morning light

149

The Man

now becomes The Uniform —

stiff and ridiculous

STALKED!

by a malicious squirrel

No room for error

i awoke early

thought it's never too late

Enforced Sobriety —

My existence here

is an unmitigated horror!

conversing

  with myself

    in guarded whispers

                Two birds playing

                  Over emerald trees

                In a pink sky

deepest blue

  through a tear in the sky

    ephemeral dawn

                Shadows wander

                like splattered ink —

                Cum to life

the fly

landing on a blade ov grass

        Heat sickness

        My cock, hard and rubbery —

        This is how to live!

lost piercing

    vanity ov lament

flesh worn away

        Ever healing —

        The final balm?

Bass strapped on

  caring nothing for the rules

 high on the Himalayas

               rolling down

            my protruding ribcage

             rivulets ov sweat

feeling antisocial —

  could it be

because society stinks?

              October bees

          hitting the wilted clover

             one last time

in the Dead Man Zone

    a carpet ov break rock

  sharp and cruel

                so many voices

           drowned in their own vulgar din —

                "Progress"

i'd rather be dancing

      NAKED

covered in fallout

                They believe

           their uniforms give them power —

              They don't.

embraced

and cultivated!

total ostracism

dead branches

all that remains

scattered

Your voice

so absent upon the wind

bears a deep sadness

making me sick

all this pretence at living —

Drugs Please!!!

lost in thought —

    a spider

  crawling up my deadlock

            and so for us

              another nite

             apart

Time

it isn't passing by

it doesn't even exist

            Darkening sky

             Grey clouds

              No sun

stench ov human waste

   track-lit hallways

      cattle

                                life in a cage

                              a greater suffering —

                                    None

after a long walk....

   can't tell you what —

      spaced the whole damned thing

                                black fly

                                fat as a lord

                                in its final days

Meditating

    at nite

   In a locked cell

                 Reality!?!

         All these years in prison —

             For Nothing!!!

never harder

   my cock

    in the morning

         all this waiting

         missed opportunities

            loss

dead leaves

  crackling in my ears

  distant voices

                                i

                    am not in compliance

Appreciation

  as i look into the sky —

    gentle breeze on my face

                  Man

                  This fukkin' life

                  Is a drag

Your opinion

   on how i choose to live?

  Eat a poxy dick!

                    so tired...

                      can't keep my eyes open...

                         where's all the crystal?

Out in the garden

  Dirt —

    Where nothing grows

                         it lay where it fell

                           the autumn leaf

sweet smell ov jasmine —

  like a week old cadaver

    in the noonday sun

                    My enemies conspire

                    My lawyers never sleep —

                      We fight to the death!

cold remembrance

  ov years long passed —

 a flushing toilet

                  These fukking cops —

                Like raccoons in the trash cans

                    ov my life

doing face yoga

and looking quite insane

in the hot shower

                              here i am

                        sick ov looking at you

                           looking at me

locked inside

   my cold thoughts

      wandering

                        Summer's gone

                         Never noticed

                         Don't care

Noonday sun —

    a great dead eye

        shrouded in mist

                too obscure

                 this reference

           to what, you'll never know

    guard tower

  watching me piss —

"step away from the fence!"

                the accusation:

                "Out ov Place", yeah

                   no shit!

marooned

   this world

a labyrinth ov Mara

                  the moon

                    so old

                      so pagan

shadow

  stretched out across the land

    unhesitant

                  black coffee —

                    on the wall

                  a picture ov my son

chill ov the morning

    without light —

my reflection

                        fond memories

                            a sprawling miasma

                                ov nothing there

eyeing me askance

    as i save the caterpillar —

        the wren

                        Tattooed bones

                    Righteously indignant —

                        My middle finger

an inverted cross

hangs on my cell door

i am Thee Anti-Bodhidharma

                         "Try to be reasonable, Caius!"

                                  What!?!

                              There IS no reason!!!

Another story told

  by the dead fireside —

Lies, Lies, Lies

                         relinquishing attachment

                              the maple leaf

                                takes to the air

Old Colony Road

   Dead End

   Nothin' goin'

                  Feedback

                    Distortion —

                  My heart

Underhanded swine!

The State Police —

Coercion and Deceit

                  Underhanded swine!

                  The State Police —

                  A Vile and Ignoble lot

learning how to hate

  i dance again

    under the black moon

                    face in the window —

                      remains

                        ov lost memories

the heroin helped

  when hope wasn't enough —

open wounds

                    Black

                    No star shining

                    Night

abandoned

 the old house on the hill

all joy is gone

                  an instinctual fear —

              it's what motivates Them

                  against Me

Spanish boys

  sing songs ov their homeland —

    On the prison yard

                  falling asleep

              with his hat pulled down —

                  the old convict

weight ov the world —

    i'm kicked back

        and don't give a damn

                the tree they cut

           was the best ov them —

              ravens nest

bone colored branches

    now litter the cold ground —

        so too my dreams

                Accused —

              Convicted —

                  Innocent.

sunny day

  it rained for hours

    all clouds

                cold wind

             creeping down my side —

                torn jacket

Waiting for their next meal

  Black birds

    In the Dead Garden

                lifting fog —

                 my sadness

                  deepens

Contemplating suicide

But not too soon —

Don't want to please anyone

visit from a friend

" i "

am an ectoplasmatic discharge

looking through the bars

i should have hung myself —

years ago

Tuesday

nothin' to do

broke my E-string

"Check 1, 2 Check!" —

   you wanna know

and i ain't fukkin' sayin'

                Angry little black bird

                   taking a shit —

                Looks like the
                Pope!

smell ov effluvium

     my sanity

        in question

                 bottle fly

            majestic in the afternoon heat

                emerald

strange looking beetle —

don't know what it is really...

but we're fast becoming friends

                              My dreams

                                   Disturbed

                                        Are all Nightmares

writing Haiku

   and ripping Black Metal

      no Common Ground between us

                              Walking the yard

                                   alone

                                        a Freak

guru bead

removed from the string

No Guru

A craving

cigarettes and port —

Indian Summer

seething with hatred

against my captors —

nowhere to run

Violence suppressed

OUT ov necessity —

This is all QUITE ill advised!

surrounded

by enemies and phonies —

alone

Greased up and filthy!

My dreadlocks!!

My LIFE!!!

a trivial argument

left a chill

which continues to endure

"Compromise"

Disloyalty to self —

Bad policy, Man!

beneath such laden shoulders

      dirt

                             silently

                             considering death

sick ov the gimmick

fukkin' humanity

simply has to end

                             Noncompliance

                    with the New Word Order —

                         A rotting skunk

cold hospital cell

  so removed from the world —

crusted in grime

                                     Pale semblance ov life

                             this grinning mockery —

                                    FUKK MY CORPSE!!!

hitching a ride

  on my arm

a ladybug

                                      Morning light

                          beyond the razor wire —

                                  Rising free

from this tomb

    none can hear

  my hallow voice

                Dead —

              i am

                  the living dead

      i —

have another cup ov coffee

and decide to lose my mind

              in my cell

               writing haiku

              cold toes

they look

i've dematerialized

they cannot see

an ant

crawling across my dinner tray —

tofu and rice

an old man

meticulously washing

his old face

another day

ripping on my bass —

calloused fingers

Zen beads

   Sans guru

   i lost count

          sepia yesterdays

         false friends

      and other transparent lies

An impeccable record

   ov Bad Behavior —

     i shall not fail!

        Witching Hour approaches

         and the shadows

         from the shadows crawl

obligations?

what do YOU wanna' do?

Slip the yoke!!!!

> When i die
>
> the change will be subtle —
>
> Wraith

keys rattling

    at their side

   abuse ov power

> cold, cold and damp
>
> my bones
>
> shards ov ice

Poor acting

    Shoddily crafted masks —

The Populace

                    this mountain...

              this mountain without a peak

  eyes open —

mind a vacuum

ov non-locality

                   abandoned

                     the stone cottage

                      seems appealing

a caustic light

  brings pain to my eyes —

"Stand for count!!!"

                so serene

          the sound ov running water —

               a broken toilet

in the garden

  fed up

i plant my shovel

              blue uniform

            starch —

              loss ov identity

clipped fingernails

   all in a neat little pile —

i want to blacken his eyes!!!

                  a thin blanket

          none but small comforts...

            "comforts" ??

WiFi is out

a skunk crosses the street

riots ensue

        in the Cold Light

      illuminating No Mans Land —

        a sentient Fear

on a roll

   in an unbroken line

   ov bad decisions

                from my cell

              looking toward the Night Sky

                  Beyond The Gates

way too cool

   with tinsel in her hair —

what was i sayin'?

                  Rainbows —

                    with accoutrements!

                  i forget everyfukkingthing.

in the distance

some trees

i never noticed before

it's night again

my skin

tightens

in the orange twilight

my spirit soars —

silver crescent moon

four walls

covered in torn out pictures

empty

One beat towel

just hangin' there on the line —

One beat towel

Late chow

Panic —

System Kollapse!

cold light

casting shadows ov dust

across the table

this isn't your reality —

dead poem

translucent ghost moon

   lingering

  above the jade trees

                October fire

            come

           and engulf us all

by the window

   staring into the gloom

     my heart breaks

            bright blue dragonfly

           on a mission —

          known only to itself

Vomit

on the floor

Feeding my flies

autumn leaves

each one

perfect

As i languish here

my rage continues to grow

Soon.... soon.

smell ov onions

no one's cooking —

pit check

Still stuck in this prison

    Lonelier than last year —

November

                              My wrath —

                              Only suffering

                    May cleanse such suffering

Carefully crafted —

    Smashed

Unceremoniously

                        this emptiness

                        augmented only

                            by you

Pentagram gleaming

   reflected

In the red lamplight

                    mind adrift

               i'm holding my erection

                    firmly

in my rack

  crankin' the Ramones

 thinkin' about you

               Skulls on The Wall

           My own among them —

               Rictus Grin

my lost hat

  outside

    leaves on the ground

         Balanced

         Upon a threshold moment —

         What was that again?

dust

  ov those who've passed before me

    in my none

         gazing out

           a deep azure sky

           filled with dishonesty

Itching

  To take a scalpel to my face!

Body Dismorphia

                my bass guitar

                  distortion

          and a heart full ov hatred

trying to piss

 my cock retreats —

grip ov winter

                too many years

           i've spent in this cage —

               tortured

Hunger

  gnawing at my guts —

Prison

                              She looked at me

                        with fear in her eyes —

                              Misplaced

old dead tree —

  a tragedy

they cut it down

                              the ravens cry

                                their favorite perch

                                felled

the old tree

  where it once stood

    empty space

            waiting for...

          i can't take much more ov this —

              Cell

an ancient stain

  grease memories

    long forgotten

            so many skulls

         each as empty as the next —

           spare me this horror

walking

in circles

into oblivion

                    Photographs

                    ov people i'll never meet

                    All in a row

what IS this place?

  some kind ov abnormal tomb —

The Dead walk!!!

                a skeletal hand

                reaching toward an empty sky —

                the dead tree

hatred

  though what's it fukkin' matter?

Scum Rises

               undecided

                 the finch

            hopping from branch to branch

eyes glazed and bulging

  dreams ov death

    awaken

                lights on

                  it's too early

                  don't wanna' get up

elderly punk

  pushing a walker

    jammin' Dead Boys

              Ah,

           setting the world on fire —

             Just for kicks

guzzling

  without restraint

  the last dregs ov wine

            on the hill

             red outhouse

            under cloudy skies

blind with fear

    lost forever —

your only truth

            security lights

            brighter than the sun

               blinding me

  dreamcatcher

    —a gift

from one departed

            on the block

              drinking hooch —

           ants swarm the gutter

Pet Cemetery

an unthinkable nightmare

let this be the end

Old Man

another sorry display

ov defeatism

irate

with the spatially unaware

and those without grace

Observing the world

i have nothing to say —

Despondency

too many sets

    ov breathing lungs —

        the planet dies

                          faint memory ov hir scent —

                              i could puke.

this decrepit road

  a most perilous journey

  into the abyss

                          in its twilight hours

                          wind-torn and naked

                              the ancient oak

Tempering my ire

consequence —

Agita

a vain pursuit

looking at yesteryears pictures —

nostalgia

waiting

for the key to turn —

getting restless

dead leaves

dead end road

dead world

grim the gate

an unwelcome apparition

hanging in the mist

the night

such a sky

as this

my social circle

a dot

no one left around

This ceaseless turning

will never last

Opium Dreams

the seat ov my mind

   a cauldron

 ov debasement

                                    breaking

                       these papers set aside

                                 to pursue onanism

   budding transgender

teasing me relentlessly —

   come back!

                                  ascending deity

                                  Nightside

                                  emissions

Polluted water

a carcinogenic bath

For all the yard birds

Trigger happy screw —

He went home

and shot himself

fruits ov my labor

my dick skin

torn and raw

this joyous

so bleak and ephemeral —

spent waiting

Bleeding eyes

　Ov a blackened Buddha

Lost in thought

　　　　　　　　　Crow feathers

　　　　　　　　　　arranged just so

　　　　　　　　　　tied to a string

Visitor

　Visiting —

Go Away!!!

　　　　　　　　jealous enemies

　　　　　　　thwarted by their own malice —

　　　　　　　　　POETRY!

skull on my shelf

   collecting no dust

      wishing it was Yours

                              a rotting branch

                        lays at the foot of the oak

next to my name

   a number —

   mark ov the convict

                              perimeter fence

                        all draped in green fabric

                            blocking my view

died in his cell

   another ghost

      wandering the corridors

                 Mudra —

                   i think i've got them mixed up

                 Legs numb

the blistering wind

   convincing me

      to distrust my friends

                  broken jaw

                hanging at a funny angle

                i never liked that guy

first light ov day

too angry to masturbate

teeth grinding

What crossed my mind

Was an unwholesome thought

gunfire in the distance

all these swine

rehearsing shooting us

My deepest intent

Unbound

To ANY "reality"!

doing what i want

   and ignoring the mess

THAT is the way

                       my rancid dreadlocks

               are stinking up the place —

                    intervention

Polluted!

   slick with living muck

my dreads

                    over Here

            is really just over There...

               only somewhere Else

Jim Jones

    They

wouldn't let him Be

                          woken up

                          my cellmate pissing

                          again

greeted

  with mock sincerity

and other veiled insults

                          When asked

                            my answer

                      Was a definitive "NO"!

Mount Wachusett

  barely visible

    in the infinite distance

                        Their songs so absent —

                         Sol ignites the horizon

                           No branches left

tears in my eyes

  for what

for the tears that fell

                        Sitting Zazen —

                       Always slightly unsure

                       ov where to lay my cock

My desire

   to wield a flamethrower —

      So urgent!

               Adjusting for pressure/pleasure

                  My erection

                     Demands room

color coded

   Identities —

no place for me here

           Sleet hits my face

         nine years on this mountain —

           Sick ov this shit!

early hours

no different from the rest

feeling contemplative

Watching the rain

Fall —

i forgot for a moment

all ov a sudden

i didn't realize —

SATORI!!!

freezing wind

i'd rather be naked

driving a tank

The old man

  Screaming

    In his sleep

                under the full moon

                  in my veins

                  i feel its pulse

sleeping pills

  and a cup ov coffee

my hard bed

                this pensive feeling —

                  the window is open

                    my feet are bare

gibbous moon

Waning —

in a veil ov mist

What is this!?!

i cannot comprehend

My existence

dreams

awaken to nightmares

which never rest

this my Crooked Path

an endless spiral

into Chaos

She

    Owns Me —

  And she knows it!

          ... everything to me

           yet i stand here

          silent

if not for Hir

  let the noose be my steed

    Om Kreem

         backward turned

       Darkness casting Shadow

        the wolf howls

absent minded

  i stand above the toilet

    pissing on the floor

                descending this mountain

             now, as a thousand times before

              my heart filled with destiny

my Pain

this "Life"

all a Mirage

                  they whisper to me

                    my daemons —

                  resplendent in black!

compassion

so beautiful

so unknown

i feel its presence

strange eyes stare back at me

from the polished glass

ov things i will not speak —

from the circle

within the triangle

A lone figure

goes not unnoticed —

Emerging from the throng

like fine punishment

   it rains and rains

  seemingly without end

                    i awoke,

              dispensing with pleasantries,

               and puked on the floor

She speaks

   in deliberate innuendos —

  My imagination?

                 IT is a misnomer

              "The reality ov things" —

                 Late February

So inaccessible

Chai Tea

and a clove cigarette

So inaccessible —

HIR

a ring

ill fitting

a burden

Approaching Danger

— pretence ov etiquette —

How utterly absurd!

"Mad as a March Hare!"

  i am — They say.

Who?

                    Bare feet, warming

                In the dim sun mist —

                    Spring Equinox

FIN

www.ingramcontent.com/pod-product-compliance
Lightning Source LLC
Chambersburg PA
CBHW051719020426
42333CB00014B/1056